PRAYERS FROM THE HEART

Also by Richard Foster

Prayer
Coming Home: A Prayer Journal
Celebration of Discipline
Richard J. Foster's Study Guide for Celebration of Discipline
Celebrating the Disciplines:
    A Journal Workbook to Accompany Celebration of Discipline
The Challenge of the Disciplined Life
Richard J. Foster's Study Guide to The Challenge of the Disciplined Life
Freedom of Simplicity

∿ PRAYERS ∿
FROM
THE HEART

RICHARD J. FOSTER

HarperSanFrancisco
A Division of HarperCollins*Publishers*

Acknowledgements begin on page 119.

PRAYERS FROM THE HEART. Copyright © 1994 by Richard J. Foster.
All rights reserved. Printed in the United States of America. No part
of this book may be used or reproduced in any manner whatsoever
without written permission except in the case of brief quotations
embodied in critical articles and reviews. For information address
HarperCollins Publishers, 10 East 53rd Street, New York, NY 10022.

Library of Congress Cataloging-in-Publication Data:
Foster, Richard J.
    Prayers from the heart / Richard J. Foster.—1st ed.
      p. cm.
    Includes bibliographical references. .
    ISBN 0—06—062847—2 (cloth : alk. paper)
    1. Prayers. I. Title.
  BV245.F654 1994
  242'.8—dc20   94—9415
                                            CIP

95 96 97 98 ❖ HAD 10 9 8 7 6 5 4 3

This edition is printed on acid-free paper that meets the American
National Standards Institute Z39.48 Standard.

To Arthur O. Roberts
Philosopher, Poet, Teacher, Writer.

Dr. Roberts taught me to value
words and to treasure prayer.

CONTENTS

Part II—**Prayers for the Journey Upward**

Part iii—**Prayers for the Journey Outward**

FOREWORD

MY WHOLE LIFE, in one sense, has been an experiment in how to be a portable sanctuary—learning to practice the presence of God in the midst of the stresses and strains of contemporary life. Some people who read my books are surprised to learn that I have never been drawn to a monastic life, as important and valuable as that way of life is. For me, the great challenge has always been to experience the reality of God in the midst of going to work and raising kids and cleaning house and paying the bills.

The grand experiment is to experience in everyday life what Jean-Pierre de Caussade calls "the sacrament of the present moment"; seeking, ever seeking to live, "light as a feather, fluid as water, innocent as a child, responding to every movement of grace like a floating balloon."

Prayer is central to this reality of ongoing interaction with God. It is the foundation of all the spiritual disciplines of engagement—the *via positiva*. Over the years this has led me into many ways of praying, including the experience of praying as my own the prayers that have been preserved throughout the centuries.

This may surprise some, especially those who assume that prayer must be spontaneous in order to stay alive and fresh. But, if we are honest, we all must admit that there are times when we simply cannot find the words to express the deepest yearnings of our heart, and at such times the prayer of another often is able to come to our aid with the words that we could not find for ourselves. At other times we do not feel up to praying, and the words of a written prayer will "prime the pump," so to speak.

Besides, we do not have to choose between written prayer and spontaneous prayer. Either/or can yield to both/and. I find that more often than not the written prayers of the ages lead me into spontaneous prayer of my own. We can come before God in both liturgical dignity and charismatic jubilee.

Perhaps the most famous written prayer is what we today call "The Lord's Prayer," actually "the disciples' prayer," which was given to the Twelve by the Lord when they wanted instruction in genuine, life-giving prayer. The "Our Father," as it is often referred to, contains all the ingredients of true, heartfelt devotion to God and can lift our spirit into the very presence of the Holy.

Also, the Psalms are a rich and frequently used source of prayer. Frequently I find that the heart cry of the psalmist "speaks to my condition," as the Quakers put it. It is little wonder that the Psalter is called "The Prayer Book of the Church."

Then too, we have the written prayers of two millennia of Christian devotion. These prayers come to us from varied cultures and span the centuries, and yet they all speak with the same voice of heartfelt devotion to God. When I pray the prayers that they prayed so long ago, I am somehow drawn into "the communion of saints."

Over the years these prayer experiences have led me, as you might expect, to prayers of my own, some of which I have written down. Hence, this little book.

Since the prayers of the Bible are readily accessible to you in many fine translations, I have not felt the need to include them here. (Though I do hope you will read them—and pray them—often.) The prayers I have written are interspersed with a variety of prayers by followers of the Way throughout the centuries. Their profound devotion "speaks truth to power," and I am sure that they will find a home in your heart as they have in mine.

Perhaps a word is in order about the use of the prayers in this book. I would not presume to know what is appropriate for you in your own spiritual development—that is something only you can determine as you build a personal history with God. Even so, it might be helpful to share with you how I use the prayers that have been written by others.

The most obvious feature of written prayer is the words, and so that is where I begin: looking at the words, reading the words (sometimes silently, sometimes audibly), getting some sense of the texture and shape of the words. Sometimes the prayers are poetic in form, other times they are decidedly prosaic; sometimes stately, other times simple; sometimes drawing near in deepest intimacy, other times falling back in awe and godly fear. Attention to the words, then, is the beginning point of the prayer experience.

Written prayer, however, intends far more than linguistic significance; it seeks to usher us into the loving heart of God. Therefore, as we pray the words, we are going beyond the words and into the reality which the words signify. Like Isaiah we are in the holy temple seeing the Lord high and lifted up. Like John we are flattened by the vision of the glorified Christ. Like the disciples in the upper room we are in intimate, life-transforming dialogue with the One who is the Way, the Truth, and the Life.

Once I begin entering into whatever experience God in his infinite wisdom knows is best for me (and knows that I can endure), I leave the words of the written prayer behind. They have served their purpose. My task now is to be attentive to the heavenly Monitor; listening, interacting, receiving. At times I may write down expressions of petition or praise, at other times I may move beyond words altogether—always I want to be in a posture of holy expectancy and holy obedience.

And, so for you. Jesus Christ, your everliving Savior, Teacher, Lord, and Friend will guide you into what you need. Pay attention to him.

My sincere hope is that as you read these prayers you will pass beyond reading and into praying. If so, the purpose of this slender volume will have been fulfilled.

Richard J. Foster
CHRISTMAS EVE, 1993

INTRODUCTION

A PRAYER OF PROTECTION

Loving Lord, as I begin this journey into a prayer-filled life,
please be with me—guarding and guiding. Protect me,
O God, from all evil.
    Surround me with the light of Christ;
        cover me with the blood of Christ;
            seal me with the cross of Christ.
    This I ask in the name of Christ.
Amen.

Prayers for the Journey Inward

These prayers focus on the transformation of the human personality. Throughout we are praying for the grace to be molded and shaped by God.

BE THE GARDENER OF MY SOUL

Spirit of the living God, be the Gardener of my
soul. For so long I have been waiting, silent and still—
experiencing a winter of the soul. But now, in the strong
name of Jesus Christ, I dare to ask:

> Clear away the dead growth of the past,
> Break up the hard clods of custom and routine,
> Stir in the rich compost of vision and challenge,
> Bury deep in my soul the implanted Word,
> Cultivate and water and tend my heart,
> Until new life buds and opens and flowers.

Amen.

*I am indebted to Carol Mullikin for the image of God as the Gardener of
the soul.*

A SIMPLE PRAYER

I AM, O GOD, a jumbled mass of motives.
One moment I am adoring you, and the next I am shaking
my fist at you.
I vacillate between mounting hope, and deepening despair.
I am full of faith, and full of doubt.
I want the best for others, and am jealous when they get it.
Even so, God, I will not run from your presence. Nor will I
pretend to be what I am not. Thank you for accepting me
with all my contradictions.
Amen.

GIVE US THAT SUBLIME SIMPLICITY

SUFFER US, O FATHER, to come to Thee.

Lay Thy hands on us and bless us.

Take away from us forever our own spirit and replace it by the instinct of Thy divine grace.

Take away from us our own will and leave us only the desire of doing Thy will.

Give us that beautiful, that lovable, that sublime simplicity which is the first and greatest of Thy gifts.

Amen.

J. N. Grou

A PRAYER IN DARKNESS

GOD, WHERE ARE YOU?

    I beg, I plead . . . and you do not answer.

    I shout, I yell . . . and get nothing.

Break your silence, O God.

    Speak to me!

        Teach me!

            Rebuke me!

                Strike me down!

                    But do not remain silent.

The God who is mute. Is that who you are?

ॐ

You have revealed yourself as the speaking God—our
communicating Cosmos.

You pointed Abraham to a city whose builder and maker was
God.

You revealed your divine name to Moses.

You spoke with clarity

    to David,

        to Ruth,

            to Esther,

                to Isaiah,

                    to Ezekiel,

                        to Daniel,

                        to Mary,

                          to Paul,

                            and a host of
                            others.

Why are the heavens made of iron for me?

❧

Job, I know, experienced you as the hidden God. And Elijah
held a lonely vigil over earthquake, wind, and fire. Me, too.

❧

O God of wonder and of mystery, teach me by means of
your wondrous, terrible, loving, all-embracing silence.

Amen.

ENLIGHTEN THE DARKNESS OF MY HEART

O MOST HIGH, GLORIOUS GOD, enlighten the darkness of my
heart and give me
    a right faith,
        a certain hope
            and a perfect love, understanding and knowledge,
O Lord,
    that I may carry out your holy and true command.
Amen.

Francis of Assisi

AN EXAMEN OF CONSCIOUSNESS

Spirit of the living God, you have been with me today,
and I thank you.
There was sunrise and sunset, and I am grateful for both.
 Family and friends are gifts of your grace.
  The creativity to envision new possibilities and
  the strength to bring them into reality are signs
  of your action in my life.
Thank you, Lord God, for being with me today.
Amen.

やと

 My little one, *I am pleased that you recognized my presence
through the day. But I was with you so much more than you knew. I
sustain you in ways you cannot possibly imagine. I love you, my child;
I will never leave you nor forsake you.*

AN EXAMEN OF CONSCIENCE

"SEARCH ME, O GOD, and know my heart; test me and know my thoughts. See if there is any wicked way in me, and lead me in the way everlasting."

꙳

God, I pray these words of the psalmist with great hesitation. They are devastatingly honest.

    They lay things so bare.

        They allow no room for negotiation or compromise. I fear the scrutiny.

    I dread the probe.

        I resist the intrusion.

I know that you are all love and so I am entering nothing more than your scrutiny of love. And yet . . .

    No! I refuse to allow my fears to keep me from your love.

꙳

"Search me, O God, and know my heart; test me and know my thoughts. See if there is any wicked way in me, and lead me in the way everlasting."
Amen.

The quotation comes from Psalm 139:23, 24.

GIVE US A PURE HEART

Give us

    A pure heart

        That we may see Thee,

    A humble heart

        That we may hear Thee,

    A heart of love

        That we may serve Thee,

    A heart of faith

        That we may live Thee,

Thou

    Whom I do not know

        But Whose I am.

Thou

    Whom I do not comprehend

        But Who hast dedicated me

        To my fate.

Thou—

Amen.

Dag Hammarskjöld

PRAYING THROUGH CHRONIC PAIN

O LORD, MY GOD, I do not ask for the pain to go away. I've prayed that prayer a thousand times over, and the pain remains with me. But I'm not angry about it. I'm not even disappointed anymore. I've come to terms with my pain.

No, my prayer is much more basic, much more simple. I ask, O God, for help in getting through this day. It's difficult because I've lost the ability to care.

God, what's hardest of all is that no one understands my experience of pain. If I had a broken leg, they could understand. But my pain is too hidden for them to understand. And because they cannot understand, they doubt my experience, and when they doubt my experience, they doubt me. And their doubts make me doubt myself, and when I doubt myself, it is hard to get through the day.

Maybe Lord, the pain is all in my head, like everyone says. Even those closest to me think that though they've learned not to say it. Jesus, do you think that too?

Meaning has long since fled my life. What purpose is there in all this pain? Why am I here on this earth? What am I supposed to do with my life? These questions mock me.

I don't know who I am anymore, but whoever I am, O Lord, you know that I am Thine.
Amen.

THE SERENITY PRAYER

GOD, GRANT US
   the serenity to accept the things we cannot change,
   courage to change the things we can,
   and wisdom to know the difference.
Amen.

Reinhold Niebuhr

A PRAYER FOR RAGE

1   *Acknowledgement*

DEAR GOD, I come to you with
an overwhelming anger,
a bursting rage.

This rage is like a cancer
shut up in my bones,
eating away at my soul.

Today, O God, I acknowledge this rage.
I do not suppress it,
or hide from it.

Thank you, Lord,
thank you
for accepting me
rage and all.

This prayer grew out of a request from a woman who, through extensive counseling, had made substantial progress in dealing with childhood sexual abuse, but was hoping for a prayer to help her through her rage. It is in no way meant to be a substitute for professional help, nor is it a quick fix. If you are working through a deep-seated rage, I urge you to take advantage of the best professional help available.

This prayer may be too much to enter into in one sitting. If so, feel at liberty to take it in small doses, allowing the Spirit to search your mind and heal your heart throughout.

O God, I feel a burning rage within.
A fire gone wild.
Burning, always burning.

God, I hate what was done to me.
It was so evil.
So wrong.

Why this evil?
Why this degradation?
Why? Why? Why?

My rage, O God, is the only power I have
against this vicious world.
That's why I cannot let it go.
Please, God, don't ask me to let it go.

III   *Turning*

God, I cannot separate
my hatred for what was done
from the person who did it.

I despise the deed.
I loathe the person who did the deed.
My rage is my only revenge.

But, God, my rage destroys me too.
I feel this seething anger
searing my own soul.

O Lord, my God,
deliver me
from the evil
I would do to myself.

IV *Forgiving*

I refuse to allow this evil
to control me
any more.

I will not be held in bondage
to my hate
any longer.

But, the strength to love,
is not in me.
I must wait for your enabling.

Now, in your great power,
and with a trembling heart,
I speak your word
of forgiveness.

v *Healing*

May your healing light shine, O God,
into every crack
and crevice of my soul.

Rage once made me feel strong.
But now I receive your light,
encircling me with love.

I have not forgotten
what was done to me.
I will never forget.

But, today I choose
to live
as your child
of infinite worth.
Amen.

ALL SHALL BE WELL

BUT ALL SHALL be well,
  and all shall be well,
    and all manner of thing shall be well.

Lady Julian of Norwich

In her Showings—*a discussion of sixteen revelations given to her by God—Lady Julian says that God, in tender love, comforts all those trapped in pain and sin by speaking these words over them.*

PRAYER IN THE NIGHT

I'M WIDE AWAKE, LORD, unable to turn my mind off. I keep going over and over the events of the day. I worry about what I said and did, reconstructing conversations and encounters in a thousand different ways. I wish I could turn my mind off. I need sleep, but it's like the accelerator of my mind is racing, racing, racing.

God, why don't you help me sleep?!

I guess at a time like this I'm supposed to feel pious and pray. But I don't want to pray; I want to sleep. Why can't I turn my mind off? I'm so tired.

సౌ

God, can't you simply induce sleep—the great cosmic tranquilizer? I guess I wouldn't want that even if it were possible. But I do want to sleep.

God, why can't I sleep? Why can't I sleep?

సౌ

SHALOM, MY CHILD, *shalom. You are anxious for many things. Rest. Rest. Rest in my love. Sleep is not necessary if you rest in my love.*

This prayer was composed in a motel room in Santa Barbara, California. It was written around 3:00 A.M.

PRAYING THROUGH LONELINESS

TODAY, O LORD, I feel the loneliness of anonymity. No one in this city knows me and no one cares. At least it seems that way. So I am left to myself and my own thoughts.

My loneliness, of course, is quite comfortable. It is not the loneliness of the truly abandoned. But perhaps it can help me enter more fully into their feelings of abandonment. O Lord, may my small experience of loneliness teach me to have fellowship with all those who are marginalized:

When I eat alone, help me pray for those who have nothing to eat;

When I walk the streets alone, help me remember those who do not have the strength to walk;

When I feel on the outside of every conversation, help me see the nameless people to whom no one pays attention.

When I speak and am ignored, help me hear those whose voices fall on deaf ears.

And whenever my circumstances are devoid of familiar voices may I always be able to hear the voice of the true Shepherd.

Amen.

This prayer was composed in Winnipeg, Manitoba, Canada, in the midst of a busy convention.

A PRAYER ON ASH WEDNESDAY

Most gracious and loving God, I seek this day to remember that I am dust and to dust I shall return.

God, why do I fear being mortal? Perhaps I think it diminishes me in your sight.

And yet . . .

the flower that is here today and gone tomorrow is no less precious to you simply because it is transitory.

the sparrow that falls to the ground is no less precious to you simply because of its frailty.

So with me. I'm precious to you even though all too soon my body will be food for the worms.

Thank you, Lord, for assuring me of my infinite worth. I can now face the real truth about myself, namely, that I am dust, and to dust I shall return. And after . . . the resurrection of the dead!

Amen.

This prayer was composed following an evening Ash Wednesday service at a small Episcopal Church in Glendora, California. It marked the beginning of my Lenten meditations from which these prayers originated.

A PRAYER OF STABILITY

BROTHER JESUS,
    you have reminded me of my need
    to anchor my soul in a place of prayer,
    a place where we can come together
    to worship the Father.
Free me from my restless activity,
    my slavery to the clock,
    my habit of bobbing along on the open sea
    when you have called me to be still.
When I consider how you consented to enclosure
    in Mary's womb,
    in a narrow manger,
    in a carpenter's home,
    on the wooden cross,
    in the bread of Eucharist,
        my heart is moved to seek enclosure with you.
Amen.

Gloria Hutchinson

A PRAYER OF RELINQUISHMENT

TODAY, O LORD, I yield myself to you.
    May your will be my delight today.
    May your way have perfect sway in me.
    May your love be the pattern of my living.

               ॐ

I surrender to you
    my hopes,
        my dreams,
            my ambitions.
Do with them what you will, when you will, as you will.

               ॐ

I place into your loving care
    my family,
        my friends,
            my future.
Care for them with a care that I can never give.

               ॐ

I release into your hands
    my need to control,
        my craving for status,
            my fear of obscurity.
Eradicate the evil, purify the good, and establish your
kingdom on earth.

For Jesus' sake,

Amen.

GOVERN EVERYTHING BY YOUR WISDOM

GOVERN EVERYTHING by your wisdom, O Lord, so that my
soul may always be serving you
   in the way you will
      and not as I choose.
Let me die to myself so that I may serve you;
   let me live to you who are life itself.
Amen.

Teresa of Avila

A PRAYER OF SELF-EMPTYING

Loving God, I choose this day to be a servant. I yield my right to command and demand. I give up my need to manage and control. I relinquish all schemes of manipulation and exploitation.
For Jesus' sake,
Amen.

I SURRENDER ALL TO YOUR DIVINE WILL

TAKE, LORD, all my liberty,
    my memory, my understanding,
        and my whole will.
You have given me all that I have,
    all that I am,
        and I surrender all to Your Divine will.
You have given me all that I have,
    all that I am,
        and I surrender all to Your Divine will.
Give me only Your love and Your grace.
    With this I am rich enough,
        and I have no more to ask.
Amen.

Ignatius of Loyola

Notice how in the middle of this prayer Ignatius speaks the words of surrender twice, as if to echo and affirm their reality.

A PRAYER OF CLEANSING

CLEAN OUT, O GOD, the inner stream of my life:
>   all the duplicity,
>   all the avarice,
>   all the falsity.

Search out, O Lord, the hidden motives of my life:
>   all the conceit,
>   all the anger,
>   all the fear.

Root out, divine Master, the destructive actions of my life:
>   all the manipulation,
>   all the scheming,
>   all the guile.

May the operations of faith, hope, and love increase in
everything I am and in everything I do.

Amen.

BE PLEASED TO CLEANSE ME

O LORD, I have heard a good word inviting me to look away to Thee and be satisfied. My heart longs to respond, but sin has clouded my vision till I see Thee but dimly.

Be pleased to cleanse me in Thine own precious blood, and make me inwardly pure, so that I may with unveiled eyes gaze upon Thee all the days of my earthly pilgrimage. Then shall I be prepared to behold Thee in full splendor in the day when Thou shalt appear to be glorified in Thy saints and admired in all them that believe.

Amen.

A. W. Tozer

A PRAYER OF TEARS

Let me enter your heart, O God.
    Let me see what breaks your heart.
        Let my heart be broken too.
Amen.

LORD, LORD, OPEN UNTO ME

Open unto me—light for my darkness.
Open unto me—courage for my fear.
Open unto me—hope for my despair.
Open unto me—peace for my turmoil.
Open unto me—joy for my sorrow.
Open unto me—strength for my weakness.
Open unto me—wisdom for my confusion.
Open unto me—forgiveness for my sins.
Open unto me—tenderness for my toughness.
Open unto me—love for my hates.
Open unto me—Thy Self for my self.

Lord, Lord, open unto me!
Amen.

Howard Thurman

A FORMATION PRAYER

O Lord, my God. Form me more fully into your likeness.
Use the circumstances and interactions of this day to form
your will in me.

From the frustrations of this day form peace.

From the joys of this day form strength.

From the struggles of this day form courage.

From the beauties of this day form love.

In the name of Jesus Christ who is all peace and strength
and courage and love.

Amen.

A PRAYER OF COVENANT

TODAY, O LORD, I say YES!
    to you,
        to life,
            to all that is true, and good, and beautiful.
Amen.

COME! SPIRIT OF LOVE!

COME! SPIRIT OF LOVE! Penetrate and transform us by the action of Your purifying life. May Your constant, brooding love bring forth in us more love and all the graces and works of love. Give us grace to remain still under its action, and may that humble stillness be our prayer.
Amen.

Evelyn Underhill

SALUTATION OF THE VIRTUES

Hail, Queen Wisdom! May the Lord preserve you
　　with your sister holy pure Simplicity!
O lady holy Poverty, may the Lord save you
　　with your sister holy Humility!
O lady holy Charity, may the Lord save you
　　with your sister holy Obedience!
O all you most holy virtues,
　　may the Lord save you all,
　　from Whom you come and proceed.

Francis of Assisi

The personification of the virtues sounds strange to modern ears. The biblical roots for this practice are found in the Hebrew wisdom literature where wisdom is frequently addressed as if a person.

A PRAYER FOR TRANSFORMATION

I PURSUE YOU, JESUS, so that I may be caught by you.
I press in so that I may know your heart.
I stay close so that I may be like you.
Loving Lord, grant me:
 purity of heart,
  humility of soul,
   integrity of life,
    charity for all.
Amen.

BATTER MY HEART

BATTER MY HEART, three-personed God, for you
As yet but knock, breathe, shine, and seek to mend;
That I may rise, and stand, o'erthrow me, and bend
Your force, to break, blow, burn, and make me new.
I, like an usurped tower, to another due,
Labour to admit you, but oh, to no end;
Reason, your viceroy in me, me should defend,
But is captived, and proves weak or untrue.
Yet dearly I love you, and would be lovèd fain,
But am betrothed unto your enemy;
Divorce me, untie or break that knot again;
Take me to you, imprison me, for I
Except you enthrall me, never shall be free,
Nor ever chaste, except you ravish me.

John Donne

*This is perhaps the most famous of all John Donne's sonnets. It is unnamed
in the original.*

II

Prayers for the Journey Upward

These prayers focus upon intimacy with God. Throughout we are praying for the grace to love God with all of our heart and soul and mind and strength.

SPEAK, LORD, FOR YOUR SERVANT IS LISTENING

SPEAK, LORD, for your servant is listening. Incline my heart to your words, and let your speech come upon me as dew upon the grass.

In days gone by the children of Israel said to Moses, "Speak to us and we shall listen; do not let the Lord speak to us, lest we die." This is not how I pray, Lord. No. With the great prophet Samuel, I humbly and earnestly beg: "Speak, Lord, for your servant is listening."

So, do not let Moses speak to me, but you, O Lord, my God, eternal Truth, you speak to me.

If I hear your voice, may I not be condemned
　　for hearing the word and not following it,
　　　　for knowing it and not loving it,
　　　　　　for believing it and not living it.
Speak then, Lord, for your servant listens, for you have the words of eternal life. Speak to me to comfort my soul and to change my whole life; in turn, may it give you praise and glory and honor, forever and ever.
Amen.

Thomas à Kempis

For the stories behind the biblical allusions see Exodus 20:18–20 and 1 Samuel 3:1–14.

A PRAYER AT DAWN

GOOD MORNING, JESUS. I greet you. You greet me. The
dawning of a new day.
   "When morning gilds the skies
       my heart awakening cries:
    may Jesus Christ be praised!"
 I thank you, Lord:
    for the stillness of a morning just begun,
       for the birds whose songs somehow continue the
       stillness,
         for the warm light that slowly and surely
         dispels the darkness,
           for the hope of new beginnings.
Amen.

The quote is the opening line of an eighteenth-century German hymn.
The authorship is unknown, but it was translated into English in 1854 by
Edward Caswall. At the time I wrote this, I was actually watching the
first light of morning dispel the darkness.

PRAYER TO BEGIN THE DAY

JESUS, I DESIRE to start this day with you. And yet, my mind
keeps flitting to so many things:

> the projects I want to accomplish,
>> the people I want to talk to,
>>> the people I wish I didn't have to
>>> talk to.

I wonder. Are these things distractions to spiritual con-
centration or invitations to see God in the ordinary? I'm not
sure. Jesus, I know that you are that Center who knows no
distraction. So I offer up my mental fragmentation to you,
O Lord my God. May my scatteredness become your gath-
eredness. As I'm contemplating a thousand things, Jesus,
may I somehow be contemplating you.

Amen.

A PRAYER AT COFFEE TIME

SOMEHOW, JESUS, I like praying with a cup of coffee in my hands. I guess the warmth of the cup settles me and speaks of the warmth of your love. I hold the cup against my cheek and listen, hushed and still.

I blow on the coffee and drink. O Spirit of God, blow across my little life and let me drink in your great Life. Amen.

Often I will allow the coffee to determine the length of my prayer time. When the coffee is gone, I am ready to turn my attention to the tasks of the day.

MEAL TIME PRAYER

THANK YOU, DEAR LORD, for food.
   I like:
      the smells
         the colors
            the tastes
               the textures.
Thank you, dear Lord, for food.
Amen.

DAY BY DAY

O MOST MERCIFUL REDEEMER, friend, and brother,
    may we know Thee more clearly,
    love Thee more dearly,
    and follow Thee more nearly,
       day by day.
Amen.

Richard of Chichester

You may recognize this thirteenth-century prayer as the text for the song "Day by Day" from the Broadway musical Godspell.

I HAVE ONLY TODAY

My LIFE is an instant,
An hour which passes by;
My life is a moment
Which I have no power to stay.
You know, O my God,
That to love you here on earth—
I have only today.

Thérèse of Lisieux

Thérèse is famous for her "Little Way" of prayer in which she would seek out the menial task, welcome unjust criticisms, befriend those who annoyed her, and help those who were ungrateful.

SEARCHING FOR FAITH

God, today I resonate with the desperate cry in the Gospel, "I believe, help my unbelief." Sometimes I think I operate my life out of more doubt than faith. And yet I want to believe . . . and I do believe.

I'm a complex creature. At times I can believe with my head, while my body is still locked into patterns of skepticism and doubt. Faith is not yet in my muscles, my bones, my glands.

Increase faith within me, O Lord. I'm sure that for faith to grow you will put me in situations where I'll need resources beyond myself. I submit to this process.

Will this mean moving out on behalf of others, praying for them and trusting you to work in them? If so, then show me the who, what, when, and where, and I will seek to act at your bidding. Throughout I am trusting you to take me from faith to faith—from the faith I do have to the faith that I am in the process of receiving.

Thank you for hearing my prayer.

Amen.

HOPE IN GOD

How, O LORD, can I have hope when this world is such an insecure place?
>Natural calamities destroy.
>>Economic uncertainties abound.
>>Human beings kill.

>>↝

>>I AM *the light of the world.*

>>↝

What, O God, is reliable? What is secure?
>Not people.
>>Not institutions.
>>Not governments.

>>↝

>>I AM *the way, the truth, and the life.*

>>↝

I fear, Lord, that evil will win out in the end.
>I worry that my efforts will be for nothing.
>>I feel overwhelmed by powers beyond my control.

>>↝

>>I AM *the resurrection and the life.*

>>↝

You alone, O Lord, are my hope. You alone are my safety. You alone are my strength. May I—even with my fears and anxieties, my insecurities and uncertainties—swing like a needle to the pole star of the Spirit.
Amen.

For the stories behind the biblical allusions, see John 9, 11, and 14.

LATE HAVE I LOVED YOU

Late have I loved you, O beauty so ancient and so new.
Late have I loved you! You were within me while I have gone
outside to seek you. Unlovely myself, I rushed towards all
those lovely things you had made. And always you were
with me, and I was not with you.

All these beauties kept me far from you—although they
would not have existed at all unless they had their being in
you.

You called,
  you cried,
    you shattered my deafness.
You sparkled,
  you blazed,
    you drove away my blindness.
You shed your fragrance, and I drew in my breath, and I
pant for you. I tasted and now I hunger and thirst. You
touched me, and now I burn with longing for your peace.

Augustine of Hippo

This prayer is taken from one of the earliest and most influential Christian autobiographies ever written, The Confessions *by St. Augustine.*

A SOJOURNING PRAYER

O Lord, my Lord, I am a stranger in a strange land. Absent are all the subtleties of custom and language and sight and smell and taste which normally give me my bearings.

Jesus, everliving Teacher, use my out-of-placeness to remind me again of my alien status in this world. I belong to another kingdom and live out of another reality. May I always be ultimately concerned to learn the nuances of this eternal reality so that when it becomes my permanent residence I will not find it strange in the least.

In the name of him who entered a foreign land so that whosoever will might come home to that for which they were created.

Amen.

This prayer was composed in the midst of an extended trip to Southeast Asia.

DEVELOP IN ME A LONGING THAT
IS UNRESTRAINED

I ASK YOU, Lord Jesus,
    to develop in me, your lover,
        an immeasurable urge towards you,
        an affection that is unbounded,
        a longing that is unrestrained,
        a fervour that throws discretion to the winds!
The more worthwhile our love for you,
    all the more pressing does it become.
Reason cannot hold it in check,
    fear does not make it tremble,
        wise judgment does not temper it.

Richard Rolle

PURITY OF HEART IS TO WILL ONE THING

FATHER IN HEAVEN! What are we without You! What is all that we know, vast accumulation though it be, but a chipped fragment if we do not know You! What is all our striving, could it ever encompass a world, but a half-finished work if we do not know You: You the One, who is one thing and who is all!

So may you give to the intellect
    wisdom to comprehend that one thing;
to the heart,
    sincerity to receive this understanding;
to the will,
    purity that wills only one thing.
In prosperity, may you grant
    perseverance to will one thing;
amid distractions,
    collectedness to will one thing;
in suffering,
    patience to will one thing.
You that gives both the beginning and the completion, may You early, at the dawn of day, give to the young the resolution to will one thing. As the day wanes, may You give to the old a renewed remembrance of their first resolution, that the first may be like the last, the last like the first, in possession of a life that has willed only one thing.

Søren Kierkegaard

A PRAYER OF ACCEPTED TENDERNESS

Today, O Lord, I accept your acceptance of me.
I confess that you are always with me and always for me.
I receive into my spirit your grace, your mercy, your care.
I rest in your love, O Lord. I rest in your love.
Amen.

The term "accepted tenderness" is Brennan Manning's. The concept is fleshed out in his book The Wisdom of Accepted Tenderness: Going Deeper into the Abba Experience *(Denville, NJ: Dimension Books, 1978).*

EUCHARISTIC PRAYER

I EAT. I DRINK. Spirit welling up unto everlasting life.
Thank you, Lord Jesus.
Amen.

This prayer was composed following a simple Palm Sunday communion service at the Aqueduct Retreat Center in North Carolina.

THE SACRAMENT OF THE WORD

Today, O Lord, I'm listening to the proclamation of the Word. Help me to listen as much with the heart and the will as I do with the head.
Amen.

BODY PRAYER

I PRAY TODAY with my head, Lord, lifting it heavenward in
adoration.
I pray today with my eyes, Lord, looking for the things that are
not seen.
I pray today with my hands, Lord, raising them in jubilant
praise.
I pray today with my knees, Lord, bowing in submission and
contrition.
I pray today with my feet, Lord, working with all my might.
May you be pleased with my prayer.
Amen.

*Romans 12:1—"I appeal to you therefore, brothers and sisters, by the mercies
of God, to present your bodies as a living sacrifice, holy and acceptable to
God, which is your spiritual worship."*

A PRAYER FOR QUIET

I HAVE, O LORD, a noisy heart. And entering outward silence doesn't stop the inner clamor. In fact, it seems only to make it worse. When I am full of activity, the internal noise is only a distant rumble; but when I get still, the rumble amplifies itself. And it is not like the majestic sound of a symphony rising to a grand crescendo; rather it is the deafening din of clashing pots and clanging pans. What a racket! Worst of all, I feel helpless to hush the interior pandemonium.

Dear Lord Jesus, once you spoke peace to the wind and the waves. Speak your shalom over my heart. I wait silently . . . patiently. I receive into the very core of my being your loving command, "Peace, be still."
Amen.

This prayer was composed while on a silent retreat in Singapore, Southeast Asia.

ABBA PRAYER

ABBA, I adore you.
    Abba, I adore you.
        Abba, I adore you.
            Abba, my Abba.

(Continue this gentle repetition until you sense completion of the prayer work.)

A PRAYER OF STILLNESS

I WAIT NOW in silence, Lord, that the good may spring up
and the evil dissipate.

May the ocean of your light continually overcome the ocean of my darkness.
Amen.

GIVE ME YOURSELF

GOD, OF YOUR GOODNESS give me yourself, for you are
enough for me. And only in you do I have everything.
Amen.

Lady Julian of Norwich

MAY YOU BELONG ENTIRELY TO GOD

MAY THE YOKE of the Law of God
    be upon your shoulder,
the coming of the Holy Spirit
    on your head,
the sign of Christ
    on your forehead,
the hearing of the Holy Spirit
    in your ears,
the smelling of the Holy Spirit
    in your nose,
the vision of the people of heaven
    in your eyes,
the speech of the people of heaven
    in your mouth,
the work of the Church of God
    in your hands,
the good of God and of neighbor
    in your feet.
May God dwell in your heart
and may you belong entirely to God the Father.
Amen.

Breastplate prayer of St. Fursa

A PRAYER FOR HOLY LEISURE

I confess to you, dear God, that holy leisure is far from me. I have a minute of empty space and I rush to fill it. I act, I do, I talk. Why can't I simply be still?

※

You need to know, my child, that I will not compete for your attention. If you choose to be distracted, I will not force myself on you.

※

O Lord, it frightens me that I could crowd you out of my life. Plant in me a longing for stillness. Create in me a hunger for open, empty space.

※

As you wish.

LET ME WALK IN THE WAY OF LOVE

O *my* GOD, let me walk in the way of love which knoweth
not how to seek self in anything whatsoever.

But what love must it be?

It must be an ardent love,

a pure love,

a courageous love,

a love of charity,

a humble love,

and a constant love.

O Lord, give this love into my soul, that I may never
more live nor breathe but out of a most pure love of Thee,
my All and only Good.

Amen.

Dame Gertrude More

A PRAYER OF WONDER

I GLORY in your handiwork, O God:
    towering mountains and deep valleys,
    dense forests and expansive deserts,
    fathomless depths of blue below and immeasurable
    heights of blue above.

When I peer into the universe of the telescope
and the universe of the microscope I stand in awe at:
    the complexity and the simplicity,
    the order and the chaos,
    and the infinite variety of colors everywhere.

When I watch the little creatures that creep upon the earth
I marvel at:
    such purpose,
        such direction,
            such design;
  and yet
      such freedom,
        such openness,
           such creativity.

O Lord God, Creator of the hummingbird and the
Milky Way, I am lost in wonder at your originality.
Amen.

THE CANTICLE OF BROTHER SUN

PRAISED BE MY LORD,
    by means of all your creatures,
    and most especially by Sir Brother Sun,
    Who makes the day and illumines us by his light:
    For he is beautiful and radiant with great splendor;
    And is a symbol of you, God most high.
Praised be my Lord,
    by means of Sister Moon and all the stars:
    For in heaven you have placed them,
    clear, precious, and fair.
Praised be my Lord,
    by means of Brother Wind,
    And by means of the air, the clouds,
    and the clear sky and every kind of weather,
    through which you give your creatures nourishment.
Praised be my Lord,
    by means of Sister Water:
    For she is very useful, humble, precious and chaste.
Praised be my Lord,
    by means of Brother Fire,
    By whom you do illumine the night:
    For he is fair and gay and mighty and strong.
Praised be my Lord,
    by means of our sister Mother Earth,
    Which sustains us and keeps us,
    And brings forth varied fruits
    with colored flowers and leaves.

Praised be my Lord,
>through those who give pardon for love of you,
>and suffer infirmity and tribulation.
>Blessed are they who endure all in peace,
>For they, O God most high,
>will be crowned by you.

Praised be my Lord,
>through our sister Bodily Death,
>From whom no living person can escape.
>Woe to those who die in mortal sin!
>But blessed are those found in your most holy will,
>For the second death will do them no harm.

Praise and bless my Lord,
>And thank him, and serve him with great humility.

Francis of Assisi

A PRAYER OF AWE

You, O eternal Trinity, are a deep sea into which, the more I enter, the more I find, and the more I find, the more I seek.

    O abyss,

        O eternal Godhead,

            O sea profound,

what more could you give me than yourself?
Amen.

Catherine of Siena

A PRAYER OF ECSTASY

Fire
God of Abraham, God of Isaac, God of Jacob,
not of the philosophers and scholars.
Certitude.
    Certitude.
        Feeling.
          Joy.
            Peace.
God of Jesus Christ.
Forgetfulness of the world and of everything, except God.
Greatness of the Human Soul.
Joy, joy, joy, tears of joy.

Blaise Pascal

Pascal notes that this experience happened to him on Monday, November 23, 1654, from about half past ten in the evening until about half past twelve. He sewed this prayer into the lining of his coat so that it would always be with him.

AN EVENING PRAYER

LORD, JESUS CHRIST, under your loving gaze I consider the activities of my day.

Thank you for:
> the warmth of the sun,
>> the affirmation of friends,
>>> the help of fellow workers.

Forgive me for:
> looking to my own interests,
>> failing to encourage others,
>>> neglecting the weak.

By faith I now enter the darkness of the night, declaring "It is well with my soul."

Amen.

"It is well with my soul" is the refrain of a hymn by the same name. It was written in 1873 by Horatio Spafford after he learned of the tragic drowning of his four daughters.

BENEATH THY TENDER CARE

O LORD MY GOD, thank you for bringing this day
to a close;
Thank you for giving me rest in body and soul.
Your hand has been over me and has guarded and preserved me.
Forgive my lack of faith
and any wrong that I have done today,
and help me to forgive all who have wronged me.

Let me sleep in peace under your protection,
And keep me from the temptations of darkness.
Into your hands I commend my loved ones
and all who dwell in this house;
I commend to you my body and soul.
O God, your holy name be praised.
Amen.

Dietrich Bonhoeffer

III

Prayers for the Journey Outward

These prayers focus upon ministry to others. Throughout we are praying for the grace to always follow God's way.

STIR ME, O LORD, TO CARE

Stir me, O Lord, to care;
    for a world that is lost and dying,
        for values that are rejected and scorned,
            for enemies that hate and malign me.
Amen.

A PRAYER AT MID-DAY

THE DAY has been breathless, Lord. I stop now for a few moments and I wonder: Is the signature of the holy over the rush of the day? Or have I bolted ahead, anxiously trying to solve problems that do not belong to me?

Holy Spirit of God, please show me:
> how to work relaxed,
>> how to make each task an offering of faith,
>>> how to view interruptions as doors to service,
>>>> how to see each person as my teacher in things eternal.

In the name of him who always worked unhurried. Amen.

GRANT ME TO REST IN YOU

O MY SOUL, above all things and in all things always rest in the Lord, for he is the eternal rest of the saints.

Grant me most sweet and loving Jesus, to rest in you
above every other creature,
above all health and beauty,
above all glory and honor,
above all power and dignity,
above all knowledge and precise thought,
above all wealth and talent,
above all joy and exultation,
above all fame and praise,
above all sweetness and consolation,
above all hope and promise,
above all merit and desire,
above all gifts and favors,
above all happiness and joy,
above all angels and archangels,
above all the hosts of heaven,
above all things visible and invisible, and
above all that is not you, my God.

Come, come. Without you no day or hour will be happy, for you are my joy, and without you my table is empty.
I shall not be silent nor will I cease to pray until your grace returns to me and you speak to me in the depths of my heart.

࿐

MY DEAR FRIEND, *I am here.*
See, I have come to you because you have invited me.
Your tears and your soul's longing, your humility and
your grief-stricken heart have moved me and brought me to you.

O Lord, I called you and longed to enjoy you, and I am prepared to give up everything for you. Let my mouth, my soul and all creation praise and bless you.
Amen.

Thomas à Kempis

ENTER MY SMALL LIFE

LORD! GIVE ME COURAGE and love to open the door and constrain You to enter, whatever the disguise You come in, even before I fully recognize my guest.

Come in! Enter my small life!

Lay Your sacred hands on all the common things and small interests of that life and bless and change them. Transfigure my small resources, make them sacred. And in them give me Your very Self.

Amen.

Evelyn Underhill

BEHIND ALL MY ASKING

Dear Father God, I feel like I ask for so many things. But you bid me ask. And behind all my asking is the deeper longing for you, Lord. I do want you above all things. I can survive if you say No to the things, but please, Father, I must have you or I die.

Amen.

OPEN WIDE THE WINDOWS OF
OUR SPIRITS

OPEN WIDE the window of our spirits, O Lord,
    and fill us full of light;
Open wide the door of our hearts,
    that we may receive and entertain thee with all our powers
    of adoration and love.
Amen.

Christina G. Rossetti

A PRAYER FOR SIGHT

I SEE PEOPLE, LORD, but they're all a blur of activity . . .
a little like trees walking about. Go here! Go there! Do this!
Do that! It's like we're all in a frantic scramble of climb
and push and shove.

I'd really like to know each person as a unique individual, Lord, not just as a consumer or a competitor. But how?
Too many people enter my day for me to pay attention to
them all.

If I cannot truly "see" everyone, Lord, may I at least see
someone. Help me to see that solitary individual . . . and for
the rest—forgive, O Lord, forgive.
Amen.

MAY I SEE YOU TODAY

DEAREST LORD, may I see you today and every day in the person of your sick, and, while nursing them, minister unto you. Though you hide yourself behind the unattractive disguise of the irritable, the exacting, the unreasonable, may I still recognize you, and say: "Jesus, my patient, how sweet it is to serve you."

Mother Teresa of Calcutta

CHRIST WITH ME, CHRIST BEFORE ME

CHRIST TO PROTECT me to-day
   against poison, against burning,
   against drowning, against wounding,
   so that there may come abundance of reward.
Christ with me, Christ before me, Christ behind me,
Christ in me, Christ beneath me, Christ above me,
Christ on my right, Christ on my left,
Christ where I lie, Christ where I sit, Christ where I arise,
Christ in the heart of every man who thinks of me,
Christ in the mouth of every man who speaks of me,
Christ in every eye that sees me,
Christ in every ear that hears me.

Breastplate prayer of St. Patrick

THE HOLINESS OF EVERYDAY TASKS

IF ALL OF LIFE is truly sacred, God, then help me see the
holiness of the everyday tasks of my life:
    cleaning house and
        laughing with friends and
            eating good food and
                sleeping through the night.
Amen.

"Give us this day our daily bread." How do I pray those words, Lord? I live in the context of abundance. I simply do not worry about where my next meal will come from.

Perhaps I should pray on behalf of those who really and truly live from one meal to the next. And I do pray for them. Yet, action on their behalf is the real prayer for the poor—prayer-in-action.

I do need faith daily, Jesus, and strength and patience and wisdom and love and so much more. And real material needs too. "Give us this day our daily baby sitter." Is that how I pray for daily bread?

Teach me, Father, a life of daily dependence upon you for all things—even for the bread that is already in the pantry.
Amen.

The context that gives rise to this prayer is the recent affluence of the Western world. Most peoples in most centuries—including our own— have had no problem praying for "daily bread" with heartfelt urgency!

PRAYING THE ORDINARY

O GOD, just as the disciples heard Christ's words of promise and began to eat the bread and drink the wine in the suffering of a long remembrance and in the joy of a hope, grant that we may hear your words, spoken in each thing of everyday affairs.

> Coffee, on our table in the morning;
> the simple gesture of opening a door to go out, free;
> the shouts of children in the parks;
> a familiar song, sung by an unfamiliar face;
> a friendly tree that has not yet been cut down.

May simple things speak to us of your mercy, and tell us that life can be good. And may these sacramental gifts make us remember those who do not receive them,

> who have their lives cut, every day, in the bread absent from the table;
> in the door of the prison, the hospital, the welfare home that does not open;
> in the sad child, feet without shoes, eyes without hope;
> in the war hymns that glorify death;
> in the deserts where once there was life.

Christ was also sacrificed. And may we learn that we participate in the saving sacrifice of Christ when we participate in the suffering of his little ones.
Amen.

Rubem Alves

A PRAYER FOR HEALING

LORD JESUS CHRIST, when I read the gospel stories I am touched by your healing power. You healed sick bodies to be sure, but you did so much more. You healed the spirit and the deep inner mind. Most of all I am touched by your actions of acceptance that spoke healing into those who lived on the margins of life—shoved aside by the strong and the powerful.

Speak your healing into me, Lord—body and mind and soul. Most of all, heal my sense of worthlessness. My head tells me that I am of infinite value to you but my heart cannot believe it. Heal my heart, Jesus, heal my heart.
Amen.

ॐ

MY DEAR PRECIOUS CHILD, *come sit with me awhile.*
Others do not value you because they do not understand. They value only the most trivial of things—power, strength, beauty, wealth, intelligence, influence. You do not need those things to gain my acceptance and my love.
I call you blessed just because you are. Come close and receive my blessing. Let your heart feel the warmth of my healing.
And now, my child, never despise what I have called blessed.

This prayer was composed while I was leading a retreat for theological students in Malaysia, Southeast Asia.

LET YOUR HEALING LIGHT SHINE

Let your healing light shine, O God.
    Give doctors unusual skill in the healing arts.
    Give researchers success in curing diseases.
    Give counselors insight and healing love.
    Give pastors discernment and tender compassion.
    Give social workers courage and boundless hope.
Let your healing light shine, O God.
Amen.

FOR THOSE WITH INCURABLE DISEASES

I HOLD BEFORE YOU, O Lord, all who are ravaged by incurable diseases. What can I say? I stammer . . . I stutter. I am not worthy to speak on their behalf.

Still, as best I can I ask, dear God. Please let these who suffer so deeply know that they are not alone. Help them sense your nearness, your care, your compassion. May they somehow experience the suffering heart of Jesus.
Amen.

IF DEATH MY FRIEND AND ME DIVIDE

IF DEATH my friend and me divide,
thou dost not, Lord, my sorrow chide,
or frown my tears to see;
restrained from passionate excess,
thou bidst me mourn in calm distress
for them that rest in thee.

I feel a strong immortal hope,
which bears my mournful spirit up
beneath its mountain load;
redeemed from death, and grief, and pain,
I soon shall find my friend again
within the arms of God.

Pass a few fleeting moments more
and death the blessing shall restore
which death has snatched away;
for me thou wilt the summons send,
and give me back my parted friend
in that eternal day.

Charles Wesley

PRAYING FOR THE WILL AND THE WAYS OF GOD

Mighty and most holy God, I have a troubling question to ask. I know I border on presumption to query the Creator of all things, but it has been bothering me considerably. Here is my question: How closely tied is your will with your ways? Your will seems filled with all goodness and light, but your ways seem filled with constant lingering and delay.

ༀ

For my thoughts are not your thoughts, nor are your ways, my ways. For as the heavens are higher than the earth, so are my ways higher than your ways and my thoughts than your thoughts.

ༀ

Yes, and that is what troubles me. I believe I want your will, but I'm not at all sure I want your ways. But if I don't want your ways, then maybe I really don't want your will. You see my dilemma.

I understand your will to be connected with peace on earth, justice, righteousness, and the like. But when I look at your timing for bringing all that about, well, excuse me for saying so, but I'm not exactly impressed.

ༀ

For as the rain and the snow come down from heaven, and do not return there until they have watered the earth, making it bring forth and sprout, giving seed to the sower and bread to the eater, so shall my word be that goes out from my mouth; it shall not return to me empty, but it shall accomplish that which I purpose, and succeed in the thing for which I sent it.

⚘

I see I must totally reorient my perspective if I am to value your ways. Rain and snow seem so weak, so ineffective . . . so slow. I want things to be impressive and strong . . . and efficient. It's the time thing that troubles me the most. Why must your children wait so long and see so much suffering before your will comes to pass?

⚘

THE LORD IS NOT SLOW *about his promise, as some think of slowness,*
but is patient with you, not wanting any to perish, but all to come to repentance.

⚘

Yes, that I can understand. The delay is out of love and respect. And I do want to enter into the sense of your cosmic patience. But it still seems like your people have been waiting for a long time. I yearn to see the kingdom in its fullness.

⚘

FOR YOU SHALL GO *out in joy, and be led back in peace;*
the mountains and the hills before you shall burst into song,
and all the trees of the field shall clap their hands.

⚘

Yes, I look for that day. Even so, come Lord Jesus.

For the context of the biblical allusions in this prayer, see Isaiah 55:8–12 and 2 Peter 3:9.

MY WILL IS TO DO YOUR WILL

Lord,

> you know what I desire, but I desire it only if it is your
> will that I should have it. If it is not your will, good
> Lord, do not be displeased, for my will is to do your will.

Amen.

Lady Julian of Norwich

A PRAYER FOR THE INNOCENTS

LORD GOD, merciful Father, care for the little ones. Watch over them in all their innocence. Guard, guide, protect.

They are so vulnerable in this world gone awry. Famine, violence, and abuse abound. They have no shield, no defense. Be their shield, O Lord. Be their defense.

El Shaddai, send your holy angels to protect the children.

Protect them as they skip down the street.
Protect them as they play on the school grounds.
Protect them as they sleep through the night.

Protect them from all physical harm.
Protect them from all emotional harm.
Protect them from all spiritual harm.

Keep them from the influence of the evil One:
    from evil friendships,
        from evil thoughts,
            from evil acts.

This I ask in the strong name of Jesus who always welcomed the little ones into his presence.
Amen.

A PLEA FOR THE DEFENSELESS

O LORD, hear the cry of the defenseless.
  The men who are defeated by life.
  The children who have no food to eat.
  The homeless who have no place to sleep.
  The prisoners who have no one who cares.
  The women who are beaten and abused.
  The unborn who are killed in the womb.
  The elderly who are shoved aside.
O Lord, hear the cry of the defenseless.
For Jesus' sake,
Amen.

A PRAYER FOR SPIRITUAL LEADERS

I PRAY, dear God, for our spiritual leaders.

   Increase in them the charism of *faith* that they might preach the Word of God with boldness.

   Increase in them the charism of *wisdom* that they might guide us into the Way.

   Increase in them the charism of *pastor* that they might always lead us with compassion and strength.

I intercede, O Lord, for our spiritual leaders.

   Grow in them the fruit of *gentleness* that they might understand our frailty.

   Grow in them the fruit of *peace* that they might be free of manipulation.

   Grow in them the fruit of *love* that they might always serve out of a divine well spring.

I plead, gracious Father, for our spiritual leaders.

   Protect them from the *attacks* of the evil One.

   Protect them from the *distractions* that render their work ineffective.

   Protect them from the *criticism* of well-meaning people.

All these things I ask in the name of Jesus Christ.

Amen.

A PRAYER FOR THE CHURCH

I PRAY TODAY, Jesus, for your bride, the Church. It must hurt you to see all our sin and rebellion, all our fighting and backbiting. It's presumptuous, I know, to think I can ever enter the ache of your heart for your children. Even so, as best I can I repent of my sins and the sins of my people. We have scorned you in so many ways:

> by prostituting our integrity for the sake of personal advantage,
>> forgive us O Lord;
> by loving our structures more than your Church,
>> forgive us O Lord;
> by disregarding those who are precious to you,
>> forgive us O Lord;
> by working as if we are the ones in charge,
>> forgive us O Lord.

Forgive. Heal. Restore.

Amen.

ॐ

MY LITTLE CHILD, *I am pleased that you would come to me in this way.*

> *Gladly I forgive!*
>> *Gladly I heal!*
>>> *Gladly I restore!*
>>>> *Welcome Home!*

MAKE US WORTHY, LORD

MAKE US WORTHY, Lord,
    to serve others throughout the world
        who live and die
           in poverty or hunger,
Give them, through our hands, this day their daily bread,
    and by our understanding love,
        give peace and joy.

Mother Teresa of Calcutta

THE CREATION WAITS

I PRAY, O LORD, for the earth. Forgive us for the waste, the destruction, the disrespect. Heal the earth, O God. Heal the earth.

Amen.

"For the creation waits with eager longing for the revealing of the children of God; for the creation was subjected to futility, not of its own will but by the will of the one who subjected it, in hope that the creation itself will be set free from its bondage to decay and will obtain the freedom of the glory of the children of God"—Romans 8:20—21.

A PRAYER AT TREE-PLANTING

Lord, it may seem odd
That I should pray here, now.
But when I plant trees
I've things to say to God.

These little trees are Yours,
You know, not just mine.
A redwood grove twelve inches tall
Is hardly anyone's at all,
I suppose, except by faith.

A man gets to wondering,
Between bulldozers and the fears
Of war, why look ahead
A hundred, even thirty years?

I don't know . . . except
As these trees grow
I hope my great grandchildren
Or someone's boys and girls
Play hide-and-seek
Among the towering trunks
And chattering squirrels.

I hope they hear beauty
In the singing boughs
And birds. I hope they
Breathe clean forest air
And find Your peace.

When my hands press moist soil
Carefully about the roots
I feel Your life and love,
I feel a world reborn.

O, God, heal the scars
Of earth with trees,
And not with snags
and thorn.

Arthur O. Roberts

A PRAYER OF SPIRITUAL WARFARE

By the authority of Jesus Christ I resist all evil powers
seeking sway within me.

> I stand against the *fear* that makes me want to manage
> and control others.
>
>> Grant me the gift of *faith,* O Lord, to overcome my
>> fear.
>
> I stand against the *greed* that makes me use others for my
> own selfish purposes.
>
>> Grant me a spirit of *generosity,* O Lord, to temper my
>> greed.
>
> I stand against the *pride* that drives me to seek inordinate
> attention.
>
>> Grant me the grace of *service,* O Lord, to conquer my
>> pride.

May faith, hope, and love have increasing sway over every
thought and action.

Amen.

PRAYER FOR THE MAKING OF A BETTER WORLD

O THOU WHO compasseth the whole earth with Thy most merciful favour and willest not that any of thy children should perish, I would call down Thy blessing to-day upon all who are striving towards the making of a better world. I pray, O God especially—

for all who are valiant for truth:

for all who are working for purer and juster laws:

for all who are working for peace between nations:

for all who are engaged in healing disease:

for all who are engaged in the relief of poverty:

for all who are engaged in the rescue of the fallen:

for all who are working towards the restoration of the broken unity of Thy Holy Church:

for all who preach the gospel:

for all who bear witness to Christ in foreign lands:

for all who suffer for righteousness' sake.

Cast down, O Lord, all the forces of cruelty and wrong. Defeat all selfish and worldly-minded schemes, and prosper all that is conceived among us in the spirit of Christ and carried out to the honour of His blessed name.
Amen.

John Baillie

FOR THE RULERS OF THE NATIONS

TODAY, O GOD, I hold before you the rulers of the nations—Kings, Queens, Presidents, Prime Ministers—all who are in positions of supreme leadership.

I can be quick to criticize: help me, Lord, to first enter their dilemma. On most issues of state I have the luxury of withholding judgment, of not committing myself, of sitting on the fence. Even when I have an opinion, it has little influence and seldom any consequence. Not so with the rulers of the nations. To the extent that they really lead, they must make decisions, even if they are poor ones.

Help these leaders, O God, in the loneliness of their decisions. Put wise counselors around them.

Take, I pray, the bits and pieces of virtue that are in each ruler and cause them to grow and mature. And take all destructive motives and cause them to vanish like smoke in the wind.

Lord, I know that many—perhaps most—rulers do not know you, nor do they seek you. But you seek them! Help them see how good right decisions are. And where decisions must be made that are not in their own interest, deepen their sense of duty. Having seen the light, give them the courage to walk in the light.

Amen.

TO DO SOME WORK OF PEACE FOR THEE

O LORD,
 open my eyes that I may see the needs of others;
 open my ears that I may hear their cries;
 open my heart so that they need not be without succor;

 let me not be afraid to defend the weak because of the
 anger of the strong,
  nor afraid to defend the poor because of the anger
  of the rich.

Show me where love and hope and faith are needed,
 and use me to bring them to those places.

And so open my eyes and my ears
 that I may this coming day be able to do some work of
 peace for thee.
Amen.

Alan Paton

MAKE ME AN INSTRUMENT OF THY PEACE

LORD, MAKE me an instrument of thy peace;
    where there is hatred, let me sow love;
    where there is injury, pardon;
    where there is doubt, faith;
    where there is despair, hope;
    where there is darkness, light;
    and where there is sadness, joy.
O Divine Master,
    grant that I may not so much seek
    to be consoled as to console;
    to be understood, as to understand;
    to be loved, as to love;
    for it is in giving that we receive,
    it is in pardoning that we are pardoned,
    and it is in dying that we are born to eternal life.

Francis of Assisi

NOTES

Part I

GIVE US THAT SUBLIME SIMPLICITY. J. N. Grou as quoted in Evelyn Underhill, *The Ways of the Spirit,* ed. Grace Adolphsen Brame (New York: Crossroad, 1990), p. 76.

ENLIGHTEN THE DARKNESS OF MY HEART. Francis of Assisi, *The Prayers of Saint Francis,* trans. Ignatius Brady (Ann Arbor, MI: Servant, 1987), p. 19.

GIVE US A PURE HEART. Dag Hammerskjöld, *Markings* (New York: Knopf, 1964), pp. 214–15.

THE SERENITY PRAYER. Reinhold Niebuhr, *The Little Red Book* (Hazelden Foundation, 1986), p. 58. Most sources will list this prayer as anonymous. A few sources credit Friedrich Christoph Oetinger (1702–1782). Charles Brown, however, corrects the confusion in his biography of Reinhold Niebuhr by arguing convincingly that the famous theologian is the source for this prayer. See Charles Brown, *Niebuhr and His Age: Reinhold Niebuhr's Prophetic Role in the Twentieth Century* (Valley Forge, PA: Trinity, 1992).

ALL SHALL BE WELL. Lady Julian of Norwich, *Enfolded in Love: Daily Readings with Julian of Norwich* (New York: Seabury, 1980), p. 15.

A PRAYER OF STABILITY. Gloria Hutchinson, *Six Ways to Pray from Six Great Saints* (Cincinnati, OH: St. Anthony Messenger, 1982), p. 38.

GOVERN EVERYTHING BY YOUR WISDOM. Teresa of Avila as quoted in Evelyn Underhill, *The Ways of the Spirit,* p. 95.

I SURRENDER ALL TO YOUR DIVINE WILL. Saint Ignatius of Loyola, *The Living Testament,* ed. M. Basil Pennington, Alan Jones, and Mark Booth (San Francisco: Harper & Row, 1985), p. 224.

BE PLEASED TO CLEANSE ME. A. W. Tozer, *The Pursuit of God* (Harrisburg, PA: Christian Publications, n.d.), p. 98.

LORD, LORD, OPEN UNTO ME. Howard Thurman, *The Writings of Howard Thurman* (New York: Harcourt Brace Jovanovich, 1984), p. 96.

COME! SPIRIT OF LOVE! Evelyn Underhill, *Meditations and Prayers* (New York: Longmans, Green, 1949), p. 48.

SALUTATION OF THE VIRTUES. Francis of Assisi, *The Prayers of Saint Francis,* pp. 339–41.

BATTER MY HEART. John Donne, from "Holy Sonnets," *British Poetry and Prose,* Third ed., vol. I (Boston: Houghton Mifflin, 1950), p. 487.

Part II

SPEAK, LORD, FOR YOUR SERVANT IS LISTENING. Thomas à Kempis, *The Imitation of Christ* (Macon, GA: Mercer University Press, 1989), pp. 55–56.

DAY BY DAY. Saint Richard of Chichester, *The Living Testament,* p. 142.

I HAVE ONLY TODAY. Thérèse of Lisieux, "The Eternal Today" as quoted in *Six Ways to Pray from Six Great Saints,* p. 88.

LATE HAVE I LOVED YOU. Augustine of Hippo, *Confessions X,* 27 (numerous editions available).

DEVELOP IN ME A LONGING THAT IS UNRESTRAINED. Richard Rolle, *Fire of Love* (Harmondsworth, England: Penguin, 1981), pp. 98–99.

PURITY OF HEART IS TO WILL ONE THING. Søren Kierkegaard, *Purity of Heart Is to Will One Thing*, trans. Douglas V. Steere (New York: Harper and Bros., 1948), pp. 31–32.

GIVE ME YOURSELF. Lady Julian of Norwich, *Showings*, from *The Classics of Western Spirituality*, ed. Richard J. Payne (New York: Paulist, 1978), p. 30.

MAY YOU BELONG ENTIRELY TO GOD. Prayer given to me by Lorna Khoo of Singapore.

LET ME WALK IN THE WAY OF LOVE. Dame Gertrude More, as quoted in *The Ways of the Spirit*, p. 59.

THE CANTICLE OF BROTHER SUN. Francis of Assisi, *The Prayers of Saint Francis*, p. 21.

A PRAYER OF AWE. Catherine of Siena, *The Dialogue*, trans. Suzanne Noffke, from *The Classics of Western Spirituality*, ed. Richard J. Payne (New York: Paulist, 1980), p. 365.

A PRAYER OF ECSTASY. Blaise Pascal, *Love Aflame: Selections from the Writings of Blaise Pascal*, comp. Robert Coleman (Wilmore, KY: Asbury Theological Seminary, 1994), p. 3.

BENEATH THY TENDER CARE. Dietrich Bonhoeffer, *Letters and Papers from Prison* (London: SCM, 1953), p. 169.

Part III

GRANT ME TO REST IN YOU. Thomas à Kempis, *The Imitation of Christ*, pp. 78–79.

ENTER MY SMALL LIFE. Evelyn Underhill, *Meditations and Prayers*, p. 18.

OPEN WIDE THE WINDOWS OF OUR SPIRITS. Christina G. Rossetti, as quoted in *The United Methodist Hymnal: Book of United*

Methodist Worship (Nashville, TN: The United Methodist Publishing House, 1989), no. 477.

MAY I SEE YOU TODAY. Mother Teresa of Calcutta, *A Gift for God: Prayers and Meditations* (New York: Harper & Row, 1975), p. 71.

CHRIST WITH ME, CHRIST BEFORE ME. *The Works of St. Patrick*, from *Ancient Christian Writers: The Words of the Fathers in Translation*, trans. and ann. L. Bieler (New York: Newman Press, 1953), p. 71.

PRAYING THE ORDINARY. Rubem Alves, *I Believe in the Resurrection of the Body*, trans. L. M. McCoy (Philadelphia: Fortress, 1986), p. 16.

IF DEATH MY FRIEND AND ME DIVIDE. Charles Wesley, as quoted in *The United Methodist Hymnal*, no. 656.

MY WILL IS TO DO YOUR WILL. Lady Julian of Norwich, *Enfolded in Love*, p. 1.

MAKE US WORTHY, LORD. Mother Teresa of Calcutta, *A Gift for God*, p. 71.

A PRAYER AT TREE-PLANTING. Arthur O. Roberts, *Move Over, Elijah: Sermons in Poetry and Prose* (Newberg, OR: Barclay, 1967).

PRAYER FOR THE MAKING OF A BETTER WORLD. John Baillie, *A Diary of Private Prayer* (New York: Macmillan, 1977), p. 109.

TO DO SOME WORK OF PEACE FOR THEE. Alan Paton, as quoted in *The United Methodist Hymnal*, no. 456.

MAKE ME AN INSTRUMENT OF THY PEACE. St. Francis of Assisi, as quoted in *The United Methodist Hymnal*, no. 481.

INDEX

Prayers . . .

that guide me into intercession

for when I am tempted by excessive attachments

to free me from competing loyalties

that help me confess my need

for when I rise in the morning

of justice and shalom